# SUCCESS THROUGH FAILURE

JUNE HUNT

HENDRICKSON PUBLISHERS  ROSE PUBLISHING

# CONTENTS

Definitions............................................. 11
  What Is Failure?......................................... 12
  What Is Success?........................................ 17

Characteristics of Those Who Fail...... 22
  How Do Different Personalities
    Face Failure? ......................................... 23
  What Does a Fear of Failure Produce?.............. 31

Causes of Failure...................................... 35
  What Are Rungs on the Ladder
    of Wrong Thinking? ............................ 36
  How Does Faulty Thinking
    Produce Failure? .................................. 40
  What Facts Make You a
    Failure or a Success?............................ 44
  What Is the Primary Cause of Failure?............. 50
  Root Cause of Wrong Responses to Failure ..... 52

Steps to Solution...................................... 54
  What Are Three Basic Needs? ............................ 59
  What Is the Greatest Failure? ............................ 63
  What to Do When You Have Failed.................. 69
  How to Change Your Focus from
    Failure to Success.................................. 71
  How to Turn Stumbling Stones into
    Stepping Stones .................................... 74
  What to Do When Someone Fails You ............. 80

*D*ear friend,

Looking at someone's life experiences to determine whether that person is a success or a failure is not uncommon. In fact, it is typical. We look at a person's resumé when we want to hire someone.

In line with such a practice, how would you classify this one particular man? Scan his resumé—his track record—and decide for yourself. Is he a success or a failure?

He grew up in poverty, spoke with a twang, and tried various occupations, such as storekeeper and surveyor.

At age 22—He failed in business.

At age 23—He was defeated for the legislature.

At age 24—He failed in his business again.

At age 25—He was elected to the legislature.

At age 26—His sweetheart died, leaving him heartbroken.

At age 27—He suffered a nervous breakdown.

At age 29—He was defeated for Speaker of the House.

At age 31—He was defeated for elector.

At age 34—He was defeated for Congress.

At age 37—He was elected to Congress.

At age 39—He was defeated for Congress.

At age 46—He was defeated for the Senate.

At age 47—He was defeated for Vice President.

At age 49—He was defeated for the Senate.

This is basically the half-century mark of his life—not a very impressive record. But what if this man lived to be 100 years old, or 90, or 80, or even 70? Perhaps his record would improve. Well, in this case it didn't. At age 56, he died a violent death, murdered by a man who hated him intensely.

In your estimation, then, how would you rate his life—a failure or a success? As it stands, the picture is dismal. Oh ... but let me add one fact that I failed to mention earlier. At age 51, this man became the 16th President of the United States of America.

His name? Abraham Lincoln.

Would you classify "Honest Abe" as a failure? *Hardly!* In fact, most Americans consider Abraham Lincoln *the most significant president*—and the most beloved—in United States history. He succeeded at preserving the Union during the Civil War, the most turbulent time in U.S. history. And he succeeded at freeing the slaves with the Emancipation

Proclamation—a monumental achievement. Clearly, just because he failed at times, he was not "a failure." Failure was not his identity.

What if Abraham Lincoln had *not* run for President? What if he had given up after his last unsuccessful Senate bid? What if he had deemed failure as his identity?

Now look at your own life, specifically at the times when you have failed. Is your failure an *act* or an *identity*? (Do you say, "I failed" or "I am a failure"?) If you feel like a failure, what would you be willing to forfeit in exchange for what you have gained? What clear victory? What character growth? What wise discernment? What eternal gain would you exchange for your failure? Would you truly benefit if you allowed yourself to be limited by your failure?

On a personal note, my closest friends know me as someone who hates to waste things. I'll use an envelope a second time, wrap leftover food on my dinner plate for "later," and pick up a penny on the sidewalk. As motivated as I am not to waste such little things, I have to work hard to make sure I don't waste one of my most valuable assets: my *failures*!

I haven't always seen my failures as friends. For years, they stalked me, slashing at my self-worth, filling me with guilt and regret. Let's face it: *personal failure hurts*! While I'd never ask God to cause my plans and dreams to fail, I've learned that, when they do, my response makes all the difference.

I've concluded that I learned far more from my failures than from my successes. Because my failures were far more painful, they taught me what was not good, what was not beneficial, and what would not work. I learned, more poignantly, *what not to do.*

Winston Churchill said, "Success is going from failure to failure without losing your enthusiasm." I'd add, "And without losing your *faith*." I want to encourage you to take time to pause, to stop and learn all the lessons you can from your failures. These lessons will be invaluable. Then, once you've grasped what the Lord wants you to learn, don't dwell on past defeats. As Isaiah 43:18–19 says, *"Forget the former things; do not dwell on the past. See, I am doing a new thing!"*

Decide now to learn from your failures. When you do, failure will not *define* you, it will *refine* you!

Yours in the Lord's hope,

June Hunt

*Never forget: Just because you fail, that doesn't make you a failure!*

# SUCCESS THROUGH FAILURE

## From Stumbling Stones to Stepping Stones

The boat is battered and tossed about on the waves. Surging water surrounds the disciples as they rigorously row their way across the lake in the dark of night. Before the voyage is over, Peter would both ride the crest of faith and be submerged under a wave of doubt. Jesus had instructed His disciples to go on ahead of Him. Now He joins them—by walking out to them on the water.

*"It's a ghost!"* They scream in terror, but immediately Jesus assures them it is He—there is no need to fear. Peter then makes a bold, if not brash, request: *"Lord, if it's you ... tell me to come to you on the water."* Jesus responds, *"Come"* (Matthew 14:26–29).

Quickly Peter climbs out of the boat and begins walking toward Jesus, literally walking on the water! Imagine the excitement—imagine the exhilaration! But a tide of fear soon sweeps over Peter when he becomes preoccupied with the blustery wind around him and he begins to sink. *"Lord, save me!"*

Peter frantically cries out. Immediately Jesus reaches out His hand and rescues him—and then rebukes him: *"You of little faith ... why did you doubt?"* (Matthew 14:30–31).

Could the Lord of nature, who also is the Lord of our individual lives, ask us the same question? Have we ever taken a giant step of faith with our eyes squarely on the Savior and then found ourselves distracted by distressing and daunting circumstances? While once engaged in the miraculous, doing great and mighty things in the strength of the Lord, have we later found ourselves drowning in doubt, fear, and distrust of the One who called us?

What can we learn from Peter, who like us, wavered between faithfulness and faithlessness? Can we really trust Jesus, no matter what? God often refers to Himself as a Rock—steadfast, immovable, a safe haven of refuge while the waves of perilous circumstances surge around us. And yet we often go it alone. Our repeated failure to trust can be likened to stumbling stones that trip us up and throw us off balance on the path to success. But God in His grace stands ready to reach out His hand and rescue us—just like he rescued Peter.

Discover, as did Peter, how stumbling stones can be turned into stepping stones and how God's heart is to teach us through our missteps of doubt to "walk on water."

"Now to him who is able to do immeasurably more than all we ask or imagine, according to his power that is at work within us."
(Ephesians 3:20)

# DEFINITIONS

Sinking was a certainty when Peter shifted his gaze from Jesus to the surrounding circumstances. Only after many such failures would Peter learn a primary lesson: *replace your fear with faith.*

His impetuous personality thrust him forward and knocked him backward. At times he succeeded and at times he failed. It was Peter who walked on water, who professed Jesus as "the Christ," and who delivered powerful sermons to the early church. But it was also Peter who rebuked Jesus concerning His death and resurrection, who denied Jesus three times, and who hastily at Jesus' arrest drew his sword and cut off the ear of "the enemy" (an act that Jesus immediately reversed by restoring the ear).

In truth, Peter needed grounding stability. He needed to be led not by personal passion but by the sustaining strength ... by the peace that comes from an assurance of God's perfect plan and presence.

He was emphatic in his proclamation—unwavering in his commitment. *"Even if I have to die with you, I will never disown you"* (Mark 14:31).

Bold words from a man who had just heard a painful prophecy from Jesus, piercing words that Peter tried his best to quickly dismiss. Jesus told Peter he would indeed deny him—not once, not twice, but three times *that very night*—before the rooster crowed twice.

Shortly after this conversation with Peter, Jesus' arrest triggered a dark chain of events characterized by chaos, persecution, and betrayal. The disciples' lives would be forever changed and Peter's die-hard devotion would fail again ... and again ... and still again.

> "'I tell you the truth,' Jesus answered, 'today—yes, tonight—before the rooster crows twice you yourself will disown me three times.'" (Mark 14:30)

▶ *Failure* means not performing up to expectations, being unsuccessful, or defeated.[1]

- Unmet expectations lead to disappointment and sometimes to despair.

- Disappointment with personal failure is one of the tools God uses to cultivate our spiritual growth.

▶ *Failure* in Hebrew is *parar*, which means, "to break, destroy, foil or make useless." [2] This word often applies to plans that fail because of outside opposition.

*"Plans fail for lack of counsel, but with many advisers they succeed."* (Proverbs 15:22)

**BIBLICAL EXAMPLE:** David experienced disappointment to the point of despair over his moral failure with Bathsheba. However, his broken and contrite spirit brought him closer to the heart of God. (Read Psalm 51.)

▶ *Failure* to act in accordance with God's will brings negative consequences.

- Undesirable consequences can lead to a self-evaluation that can result in a changed heart and life.

- Consequences are used by God as discipline to accomplish His ultimate will and purpose for our lives.

*"No discipline seems pleasant at the time, but painful. Later on, however, it produces a harvest of righteousness and peace for those who have been trained by it."* (Hebrews 12:11)

**BIBLICAL EXAMPLE:** Jonah's failure to obey God resulted in very difficult consequences. When running from God's call to preach repentance to a city repugnant to Jonah, he was swallowed by a great fish. In his distress, he was willing to obey. God used these consequences to accomplish His ultimate purpose of saving the people of Nineveh through Jonah's preaching. (Read the book of Jonah.)

## The Two Types of Failure

▶ *Destructive Failure:* Reveals your limitations and weaknesses, highlights your shortcomings, and when not processed correctly, keeps you feeling inadequate and defective.

**Example:**

*"When Judas, who had betrayed him, saw that Jesus was condemned, he was seized with remorse and returned the thirty silver coins to the chief priests and the elders. 'I have sinned,' he said, 'for I have betrayed innocent blood.' 'What is that to us?' they replied. 'That's your responsibility.' So Judas threw the money in the temple and left. Then he went away and hanged himself."* (Matthew 27:3–5)

▶ ***Productive Failure:*** Reveals your limitations and weaknesses, highlights your erroneous thinking, and when processed correctly, leads you to better options and keeps you dependent on the Lord.

Unlike Judas, catastrophic failure would not be the end of Peter's story.

*"Then Peter remembered the word Jesus had spoken: 'Before the rooster crows, you will disown me three times.' And he went outside and wept bitterly."* (Matthew 26:75)

## God's Heart on Failure

▶ **If you fail to let God initiate your plans**, you will find that your plans will fail.

*"If their purpose or activity is of human origin, it will fail."* (Acts 5:38)

▶ **If you fail to do what you know is right**, you are sinning against the Lord Himself.

*"Anyone, then, who knows the good he ought to do and doesn't do it, sins."* (James 4:17)

▶ **If you fail to forgive through the grace of God**, a root of bitterness will grow.

*"See to it that no one misses the grace of God and that no bitter root grows up to cause trouble and defile many."* (Hebrews 12:15)

▶ **If you fail to live with your faith placed in Christ**, you allow Satan to damage your life.

*"Simon, Simon, Satan has asked to sift you as wheat. But I have prayed for you, Simon, that your faith may not fail. And when you have turned back, strengthen your brothers."* (Luke 22:31–32)

▶ **If you fail to enter the "rest" of Christ**, you will not have the peace of Christ.

*"Since the promise of entering his rest still stands, let us be careful that none of you be found to have fallen short of it."* (Hebrews 4:1)

He consistently is listed first among the apostles and arguably could be considered the primary, predominant disciple.

*Powerful. Persuasive.* Such esteem might hint at near perfection, but Peter's life was punctuated by failure. Although he stumbled many a time, by God's grace he got up and continued his spiritual walk time and time again. His stumbling stones became stepping stones for the greater glory of God.

▶ *Success* means "achieving," attaining or accomplishing what is desired." [3]

- Succeed: "to follow another, to turn out well, to have success"

- Success: "a favorable result, a desired ending"

▶ *Success* in the eyes of the world is the accumulation of:

- Possessions—power

- Position—popularity

However, the Bible cautions us about prioritizing the earthly above the heavenly.

*"Do not love the world or anything in the world. If anyone loves the world, the love of*

*the Father is not in him. For everything in the world—the cravings of sinful man, the lust of his eyes and the boasting of what he has and does—comes not from the Father but from the world."* (1 John 2:15–16)

▶ **Success** (the word) comes from the Hebrew *sakal*, which means to be wise. [4]

- The root of the Hebrew word *sakal* means "to be wise, to have insight."

- It can also be used to indicate causing something—meaning, "to prove to be wise, to succeed." To the Hebrew, when people *succeed*, they prove that they are *wise* and have *insight*!

*"Be strong and very courageous. Be careful to obey all the law my servant Moses gave you; do not turn from it to the right or to the left, that you may be successful wherever you go."* (Joshua 1:7)

## The Two Types of Success

▶ *Pride-producing success* focuses on your gifts and abilities and brings glory to you rather than to God. Because people loved to have their gifts to the needy accompanied by the sound of trumpets, Jesus admonished ...

*"Be careful not to do your 'acts of righteousness' before men, to be seen by them. If you do, you will have no reward from your Father in heaven."* (Matthew 6:1)

▶ *Humility-producing success* focuses on the power and grace of God and brings glory to Him rather than to you. Because David, as a young shepherd boy, slew a fearsome giant in the strength of the Lord, he is a poignant example for the following Scripture:

*"Let your light shine before men, that they may see your good deeds and praise your Father in heaven."* (Matthew 5:16)

▶ **If you put your trust in the Lord, you will be led by the Lord.**

*"Trust in the Lord with all your heart and lean not on your own understanding; in all your ways acknowledge him, and he will make your paths straight."* (Proverbs 3:5–6)

▶ **If you rely on God's Word throughout your life, you will conquer sin in your life.**

*"I have hidden your word in my heart that I might not sin against you."* (Psalm 119:11)

▶ **If you live in dependence on Christ, you will receive strength from Christ.**

*"I can do everything through him who gives me strength."* (Philippians 4:13)

▶ **If your "life source" is Christ, you will bear much fruit throughout your life.**

*"Remain in me, and I will remain in you. No branch can bear fruit by itself; it must remain in the vine. Neither can you bear fruit unless you remain in me."* (John 15:4)

▶ **If you rely on Christ's power for your life, you will be godly throughout your life.**

*"His divine power has given us everything we need for life and godliness through our knowledge of him who called us by his own*

*glory and goodness. Through these he has given us his very great and precious promises, so that through them you may participate in the divine nature and escape the corruption in the world caused by evil desires."* (2 Peter 1:3–4)

▶ **If you bear the burdens of others in the name of Christ, you will fulfill the Law of Christ.**

*"Carry each others burdens, and in this way you will fulfill the law of Christ."* (Galatians 6:2)

▶ **If you live a humble life, you will receive God's grace throughout your life.**

*"He gives us more grace. That is why Scripture says: 'God opposes the proud but gives grace to the humble.'"* (James 4:6)

# CHARACTERISTICS OF THOSE WHO FAIL

Put yourself in Peter's place—just for a moment. Imagine receiving divine revelation from God the Father that Jesus is actually *"the Christ, the Son of the living God"* (Matthew 16:16). When Peter verbalizes this, Jesus calls him *"blessed."*

Jesus then begins to reveal to the disciples all He will have to endure as *the Christ,* including His death and resurrection. But Peter, the recipient of that divine revelation, is transformed into a tool of the enemy. He takes Jesus aside and begins to rebuke Him. *"Never, Lord! ... This shall never happen to you!"*

In turn, Jesus rebukes Peter—in the strongest terms possible. *"Get behind me, Satan! You are a stumbling block to me; you do not have in mind the things of God, but the things of men"* (Matthew 16:22–23).

Peter must have been stunned. How could he have failed so miserably that he had lost the confidence of his Christ?

# HOW DO Different Personalities Face Failure?

The apostle Peter failed not once, not twice, but *repeatedly* and on numerous occasions.

"Failure" is a reality we all want to avoid—usually at all costs. Then why doesn't God just eliminate failure? For Him to do so would not only save us wasted energy but would also enhance God's reputation. What a simple solution—since He is all powerful, why not? Obviously God's solution to the failure factor is not to rid us of the possibility of failure, but rather to refine us through its fiery furnace.

Unless we learn to see failure from God's point of view, we can become quickly discouraged and feel the heat of defeat. The Lord allowed four of His most prominent servants—Peter, Paul, Abraham, and Moses—to experience the pain and humility of great failure in order to reveal their true character and refine them for future service.

> "See, I have refined you,
> though not as silver; I have tested
> you in the furnace of affliction."
> (Isaiah 48:10)

### #1 Personable Peter—The Most *Devastated* by Failure[5]

Following the arrest of Jesus, Peter denied even knowing Christ. Prior to the arrest of Jesus, Peter had been boastful and proud in proclaiming loyalty to his Lord. Then as Jesus was being arrested, Peter had been extremely aggressive and had taken matters into his own hands. Ultimately, when Peter realized that he had failed three tests of faithfulness, he was devastated. (Read Matthew 26:31–45 and 69–75.)

*"Peter replied, 'Man, I don't know what you're talking about!' Just as he was speaking, the rooster crowed. The Lord turned and looked straight at Peter. Then Peter remembered the word the Lord had spoken to him: 'Before the rooster crows today, you will disown me three times.' And he went outside and wept bitterly."* (Luke 22:60–62)

#### ▶ *Basic Personality Flaws*

- Inconsistent

- Undisciplined

- Impulsive

▶ *Basic Personality Fears*

- Failure
- Rejection
- Poor performance

▶ *But Later*

When Peter finally turned from fear to faith, his public proclamation of how to have a life-changing relationship with Jesus resulted in the salvation of thousands of people.

*"With many other words he warned them; and he pleaded with them, 'Save yourselves from this corrupt generation.' Those who accepted his message were baptized, and about three thousand were added to their number that day."* (Acts 2:40–41)

#2 **Amiable Abraham—The Most *Disturbed* by Failure**

Childless, Abraham on two separate occasions presented his wife as his "sister" in order to avoid conflict with two different rulers. (See Genesis chapter 12 and Genesis chapter 20.) Neither time did Abraham have his trust in God, who had promised Abraham countless descendants. Consequently, both times brought damaging consequences to Abraham—strained relationships with both rulers and discredit to the reputation of the Lord. God blessed neither of these deceptions. Abraham had said to his wife, Sarah,

*"Say you are my sister, so that I will be treated well for your sake and my life will be spared because of you."* (Genesis 12:13)

## ▶ *Basic Personality Flaws*

- Indecisive
- Overly cautious
- Self-protective

## ▶ *Basic Personality Fears*

- Conflict Making a wrong decision
- Disruptions

## ▶ *But Later*

When Abraham finally turned from fear to faith, he learned to trust the heart of the Lord and obey God's every word. Even when God tested Abraham, telling him to *sacrifice* his beloved son, Isaac, Abraham obeyed every word, even up until the last moment, at which time God spared Isaac's life. As a result, the Lord bestowed (for the second time) an unimaginable blessing upon Abraham as He spoke these words from heaven:

*"I will swear by myself, declares the LORD, that because you have done this and have not withheld your son, your only son, I will surely bless you and make your descendants as numerous as the stars in the sky and as the sand on the seashore. Your descendants will take possession of the cities of their enemies, and through your offspring all nations on earth will be blessed, because you have obeyed me."* (Genesis 22:16–18)

### #3 Melancholy Moses—The Most *Fearful* of Failure

God called Moses to a position of great leadership, yet Moses had such fear of failure that he tried to persuade God that he was incapable of the task. Moses feared the people, expressed a lack of confidence in his abilities, and pleaded with God to send someone else. (Read Exodus chapters 3–5.)

*"Moses said to God, 'Who am I, that I should go to Pharaoh and bring the Israelites out of Egypt?'"* (Exodus 3:11)

## ▶ *Basic Personality Flaws*

- Perfectionist

- Moody

- Suspicious

## ▶ *Basic Personality Fears*

- Criticism

- Rejection

- Making wrong decisions

## ▶ *But Later*

When Moses finally turned from fear to faith, he confronted Pharaoh ten times and led the Israelites—a throng of 2 million people—out of Egyptian bondage, in which they had lived for 430 years. Following their successful Exodus, Moses took no personal credit, but rather gave full glory to the Lord.

*"The LORD is my strength and my song; he has become my salvation. He is my God, and I will praise him, my father's God, and I will exalt him. ... In your unfailing love you will lead the people you have redeemed. In your strength you will guide them to your holy dwelling."* (Exodus 15:2, 13)

## #4 Powerhouse Paul—The Most *Unforgiving* of Failure

Paul had been critical of young John Mark for leaving a previous mission trip (probably because of his youth and homesickness). He now feared Mark's lack of dedication and refused to take him along with him and Barnabas on a second trip. Barnabas so disagreed with Paul's strong-willed stance that it caused a temporary rift between the two prominent early church missionaries. (Read Acts 15:36–41.)

*"Barnabas wanted to take John, also called Mark. ... They had such a sharp disagreement that they parted company. Barnabas took Mark and sailed for Cyprus, but Paul chose Silas and left." (Acts 15:37, 39–40)*

### ▶ *Basic Personality Flaws*

- Domineering
- Strong-willed
- Inconsiderate

### ▶ *Basic Personality Fears*

- Loss of independence
- Loss of respect
- Loss of power

### ▶ But Later

When Paul finally moved from fear to faith, the Lord gave him an increased sensitivity and appreciation for John Mark, as shown in these words:

*"Only Luke is with me. Get Mark and bring him with you, because he is helpful to me in my ministry."* (2 Timothy 4:11)

What can happen in *our* lives when we move from fear to faith? What great feats might God accomplish through us as He did with these four tried and proven true servants?

We should be exceedingly thankful that our God focuses on the "but later," that He sees what we can be and doesn't give up on us. It is often said that He is the God of second, third, fourth chances, and so on. This is a testimony to the immeasurable depth of His mercies and should serve as an encouragement to all of us who have stumbled on the journey.

*"The steadfast love of the LORD never ceases; his mercies never come to an end; they are new every morning; great is your faithfulness."* (Lamentations 3:22-23 ESV)

It is a chilly, foreboding night, and while Jesus stands before the high priest for questioning, Peter waits in a nearby courtyard warming himself over a fire. A servant girl associates Peter with Jesus—and *so it begins.*

Peter denies any such association, adding, *"I don't know or understand what you're talking about"* (Mark 14:68). The servant girl points a finger again, *and once again*, Peter denies being with Jesus. Somewhere in the distance, a rooster crows.

Soon some bystanders try to link Peter with Jesus and the disciples, and this time he is vehement in his response: *"He began to call down curses on himself, and he swore to them, 'I don't know this man you're talking about'"* (Mark 14:71).

The rooster's second crow had reverberated across the courtyard and had echoed hauntingly in Peter's mind. Then he remembered Jesus' prophetic words, *"and he broke down and wept"* (Mark 14:72).

Fear of failure manifests itself in various ways in different personalities.

But one thing is for certain: The fear of failure is never *constructive*—it's always *destructive*, crippling us from experiencing God's very best for our lives. And nothing sabotages our faith faster than fear, as it diverts our focus from God's power and magnifies our weaknesses. The Bible is filled with role models who faced the fear of failure by placing their faith in God. As a result, their weaknesses were turned into strengths. Be encouraged as we read about those who allowed faith to prevail, as described by the writer of Hebrews:

**"And what more shall I say?
I do not have time to tell about Gideon, Barak, Samson, Jephthah, David, Samuel and the prophets, who through faith conquered kingdoms, administered justice, and gained what was promised; who shut the mouths of lions, quenched the fury of the flames, and escaped the edge of the sword; whose weakness was turned to strength."
(Hebrews 11:32-34)**

If you recognize any of the following characteristics in yourself or someone you care about, ask God for a powerful transformation from fear to faith.

▶ *Paralysis*—failing to take any action or make any decisions for fear of being wrong

▶ *Purposelessness*—moving from one job or profession to another with no real sense of commitment or direction for fear of making a wrong decision

▶ *Perfectionism*—doing only those things that can be done flawlessly, those that carry little or no risk of failure, for fear of criticism

▶ *Pride*—refusing to engage in certain activities for fear of being less than the best and feeling inferior to someone else

▶ *Paranoia*—distrusting the motives of those who ask you to do things for fear of being exposed as being less than adequate

▶ *Procrastination*—putting off tackling an assignment or performing a task for fear of doing it poorly

When you know the depth and breadth of the love the Father has for you, your fear will dissipate and its power over you will be broken. Failure and success will take on a whole new meaning, and you will no longer be ruled by the fear of negative results. When you act in faith, you can leave the results to God, who never fails.

"There is no fear in love.
But perfect love drives out fear,
because fear has to do with punishment.
The one who fears is not made
perfect in love."
(1 John 4:18)

# CAUSES OF FAILURE

He gets in the way again! Peter, with his impetuous behavior, attempts to interrupt the Father's plan for the Son. Peter cannot possibly see how the death of Jesus would accomplish anything good or positive. In fact, *His death* seemed to be the death of the disciples' dreams.

Previously, Peter had rebuked Jesus for even talking about being crucified. Now in the Garden of Gethsemane, he tries to block Jesus' arrest, the triggering event that would lead to the Crucifixion, by using violence. With sword in hand, Peter strikes off the right ear of the high priest's servant. Immediately Jesus picks up the ear and fully restores it.

Obviously Peter didn't "get it." He failed to see the big picture—even though Jesus had tried to tell him. But Peter wasn't listening.

**"Jesus commanded Peter,
'Put your sword away! Shall I not drink
the cup the Father has given me?'"
(John 18:11)**

With Peter or with any of us, wrong assumptions always lead to wrong conclusions. All inventors are well aware of the mockers and scoffers—those who just don't "get it." But if our mind-set is correct, we won't be controlled by naysayers. We'll press forward with God's perfect plan, even if it may not make sense at the time. Stopping short means missing out on the best part of all, which for Jesus, was *resurrection*!

In 1978 the first successful transatlantic balloon flight was accomplished by the *Double Eagle II*. It was not the first attempt. In fact, thirteen attempts had been made from 1873 through 1978. What was the difference? *Lessons from previous failures!*

Success can be defined as the intelligent application of failure. Failure is a fact of life. It can lead to despair—or it can lead to increased efforts with the possibility of success.

Steps to success are usually marked with many failures. That is why your attitude regarding failures will greatly influence your future.

The result of wrong thinking often manifests itself in fearfulness.

▶ *Fearful of Ridicule*

- "They'll make fun of me if I fail."

People laughed at Robert Fulton's strange, smoking craft chugging down the river, yet "Fulton's Folly" became the first steamboat in 1807.[6]

▶ *Fearful of Inexperience*

- "No one will believe in me."

When the great tenor Caruso first sang for his instructor, he was told that his voice sounded like "wind whistling through the window."[7]

▶ *Fearful of Failure*

- "I told you I would blow it."

Albert Einstein failed his university entrance exams on his first attempt.[8]

▶ *Fearful of Inadequacy*

- "I shouldn't try. I may not know everything I need to know."

The first car Henry Ford invented and marketed did not have a reverse gear.[9]

### ▶ *Fearful of Change*

- "It's never been done—it won't work."

The Wright Brothers first offered their flying machine to the United States government but were not taken seriously. A few years later they closed a contract with the United States Department of War for the first military airplane.[10]

### ▶ *Lacking Confidence*

- "I don't think I can do it."

Babe Ruth struck out 1,330 times, but he also hit 714 home runs.[11]

### ▶ *Lacking Conviction*

- "It really doesn't matter that much."

Thomas Edison had over 1,000 failures before he found the right combination for the light bulb.[12]

### ▶ *Lacking Perseverance*

- "I can't run the risk of failure."

R. H. Macy failed seven times in retailing before his New York store was a success.[13]

## ▶ *Lacking Trust in God*

- "I really don't have what it takes."

When the great pianist Paderewski first chose to study the piano, his music teacher told him his hands were much too small to master the keyboard.[14]

> **"God did not give us a spirit
> of timidity, but a spirit of power,
> of love and of self-discipline."
> (2 Timothy 1:7)**

He is *right* in his motives but *wrong* in his timing. Peter is in an exclusive group of three, along with James and John, who are led by Jesus up a mountain for a glimpse into the heavenly realm. Suddenly, Jesus is transfigured before them, His face shining like the sun and His clothes becoming white as light. He begins talking, not with the trio of disciples, but with Moses and Elijah!

Peter concludes that the fulfillment of the kingdom has now come and begins making preparations in conjunction with its arrival. *"Peter said to Jesus, 'Lord, it is good for us to be here. If you wish, I will put up three shelters—one for you, one for Moses and one for Elijah'"* (Matthew 17:4).

The Father interrupts Peter from a voice in a bright cloud, expressing love and pleasure toward his Son, Jesus, and evoking great fear in the disciples. Jesus touches them and tells them not to be afraid. When they get up, after falling prostrate in fear, they are alone with Jesus. Obviously, there is "kingdom work" yet to do. Because Peter has faulty thinking, he therefore has faulty conclusions.

# Faulty Thinking Test

Answer the questions below to determine whether you are telling yourself lies about failure.

▶ Do you think you must avoid the hurt that results from having failed?

**Truth:** Hurt cannot be avoided in life. It gives opportunity for mental, emotional, and spiritual growth.

▶ Do you think taking "chances" almost always leads to calamity?

**Truth:** Taking chances can lead to opportunity.

▶ Do you think it is imperative to do only what is "safe," that which is within your comfort zone?

**Truth:** Your concern for safety should be secondary to following God's leading, following your heart, and satisfying your desire to grow and learn.

▶ Do you think it would be terrible if you made a wrong decision?

**Truth:** Every wrong decision can teach you something of value and can be a stepping stone to making right decisions.

▶ Do you think you must never make a mistake?

**Truth:** Mistakes are common to everyone.

▶ Do you think God will reject you or be angry with you if you fail?

**Truth:** God knows you will fail and is pleased with your fortitude and persistent acceptance of challenges that stretch your abilities and strengthen your reliance on Him.

▶ Do you think failure is an indication that you are stupid or weak?

**Truth:** Failure is universal, experienced by both the literate and the illiterate, the strong and the weak.

▶ Do you think others will think less of you if you fail at something?

**Truth:** Others value you for your character traits and Christlike attitudes and actions rather than whether or not you fail at something. And remember, they, too, have failed.

▶ Do you think it is a bad reflection on Christ when you fail?

**Truth:** Your failures provide a platform to show others that your security is in Christ, not in your successes.

▶ Do you think failure is shameful and sinful?

**Truth:** Failing does not make you a failure. Failure is sinful only when it is a result of disobedience.

▶ Do you think you must plan every action and, thus, avoid loss, pain, or disgrace?

**Truth:** You cannot control life, but you can trust the sovereignty of God when He allows loss, pain, and even disgrace in your life.

"'My thoughts are not your thoughts,
neither are your ways my ways,'
declares the Lord. 'As the heavens are
higher than the earth,
so are my ways higher than your ways
and my thoughts than your thoughts.'"
(Isaiah 55:8–9)

Following a serious failure, what makes one person continue to fail and another to become a success? The answer is twofold: Who is willing to take responsibility for the failure? Who learns the valuable lessons that can come from the failure?

Peter becomes a success because his brashness is replaced with a heart of humility. He is able to say to fellow sufferers from his own experience, *"Humble yourselves, therefore, under God's mighty hand, that he may lift you up in due time"* (1 Peter 5:6).

Success through failure. The same words can be said about Peter's spiritual counterpart, the apostle Paul. Prideful Paul learned this lesson well: Take responsibility for the wrong and gain a heart of humility.

He writes ...

**"Be completely humble and gentle; be patient, bearing with one another in love" (Ephesians 4:2).**

## The Apostle Paul

**Facts about Paul that could have *caused*
him to see himself as a failure:**

▶**Fact:** He labeled himself the worst of
sinners.

*"Here is a trustworthy saying that deserves
full acceptance: Christ Jesus came into the
world to save sinners—of whom I am the
worst."* (1 Timothy 1:15)

▶**Fact:** He strongly embraced and actively
promoted wrong priorities and values in
his young adulthood.

*"I consider everything a loss compared to
the surpassing greatness of knowing Christ
Jesus my Lord, for whose sake I have lost all
things. I consider them rubbish, that I may
gain Christ."* (Philippians 3:8)

▶**Fact:** His life was filled with
disappointments, trials, and hardships.

*"Five times I received from the Jews the
forty lashes minus one. Three times I was
beaten with rods, once I was stoned."*
(2 Corinthians 11:24–25)

▶ **Fact:** He did not consider himself to be an eloquent orator.

*"I came to you in weakness and fear, and with much trembling. My message and my preaching were not with wise and persuasive words."* (1 Corinthians 2:3–4)

▶ **Fact:** His prayers were not always answered according to his desires.

*"To keep me from becoming conceited because of these surpassingly great revelations, there was given me a thorn in my flesh, a messenger of Satan, to torment me. Three times I pleaded with the Lord to take it away from me. But he said to me, 'My grace is sufficient for you, for my power is made perfect in weakness.'"* (2 Corinthians 12:7–9)

▶ **Fact:** He was hindered by an unpleasant bodily ailment.

*"It was because of an illness that I first preached the gospel to you."* (Galatians 4:13)

▶ **Fact:** He experienced resentment and rejection.

*"After many days had gone by, the Jews conspired to kill him, but Saul learned of their plan."* (Acts 9:23–24)

▶ **Fact:** He was imprisoned and kept in chains for his faith.

*"Remember Jesus Christ, raised from the dead, descended from David. This is my gospel, for which I am suffering even to the point of being chained like a criminal."* (2 Timothy 2:8–9)

**Facts about Paul that *prevented* him from considering himself a failure:**

▶ **Fact:** He realized that God was the source of his strength.

*"We have this treasure in jars of clay to show that this all-surpassing power is from God and not from us."* (2 Corinthians 4:7)

▶ **Fact:** He refused to allow circumstances to crush his heart or control his life.

*"We are hard pressed on every side, but not crushed."* (2 Corinthians 4:8)

▶ **Fact:** He trusted God and accepted his own limited understanding of all of God's plans and purposes.

*"[We are] perplexed, but not in despair."* (2 Corinthians 4:8)

▶ **Fact:** He knew that God was with him in the midst of tough and trying times.

*"[We are] persecuted, but not abandoned."* (2 Corinthians 4:9)

▶ **Fact:** He understood and fully embraced the fact that Jesus had called him to suffer in order that the good news of the Savior would be advanced.

*"[We are] struck down, but not destroyed."* (2 Corinthians 4:9)

▶ **Fact:** He knew that things are not always as they appear and that according to God's standard, he was strongest whenever he appeared to be weakest.

*"For Christ's sake, I delight in weaknesses, in insults, in hardships, in persecutions, in difficulties. For when I am weak, then I am strong."* (2 Corinthians 12:10)

▶ **Fact:** He had learned from experience and his knowledge of the character of God that his joy was in God, not in his so-called successes.

*"I know what it is to be in need, and I know what it is to have plenty. I have learned the secret of being content in any and every situation, whether well fed or hungry, whether living in plenty or in want."* (Philippians 4:12)

▶ **Fact:** He knew his life was hidden in Christ and that whether he lived or died, whether he was considered a success or a failure, he was loved by God.

*"I have been crucified with Christ and I no longer live, but Christ lives in me. The life I live in the body, I live by faith in the Son of God, who loved me and gave himself for me."* (Galatians 2:20)

*Cocksure* of himself—that's what he is! Peter proclaims his undying loyalty to Jesus only to betray Him hours later. He then is flabbergasted at his own failure, and the characteristic cocky spirit is replaced with a crushed spirit.

It is amazing how little we know about ourselves. God has to take us through all kinds of failures to reveal the self-focused *pride* that lies dormant in the corners of our character. The only way we can be of any use to God is to respond with discernment to our disappointments. Discernment leads us to truth—and truth punctures our *pride,* all for His purpose of molding us to the image of His Son.

> "Consider it pure joy, my brothers,
> whenever you face trials of many kinds,
> because you know that the testing
> of your faith develops perseverance.
> Perseverance must finish its work
> so that you may be mature and complete,
> not lacking anything."
> (James 1:2–4)

The following acrostic of the word PRIDE can help you discern the truth about yourself. Are you ...

## Preoccupied with the opinions of others?

*"They loved praise from men more than praise from God."* (John 12:43)

## Refusing wise counsel?

*"Plans fail for lack of counsel, but with many advisers they succeed."* (Proverbs 15:22)

## Ignoring the power of prayer?

*"You want something but don't get it. You kill and covet, but you cannot have what you want. You quarrel and fight. You do not have, because you do not ask God."* (James 4:2)

## Depending on self-effort?

*"Are you so foolish? After beginning with the Spirit, are you now trying to attain your goal by human effort?"* (Galatians 3:3)

## Expecting praise and personal recognition?

*"Everyone who exalts himself will be humbled, and he who humbles himself will be exalted."* (Luke 14:11)

With absolute confidence he crows, "I would never do that! I would never stoop to that. I'm stronger than that!"

Then the day comes when the very act he said he wouldn't do, he does. And sadly, not just once. Here is Peter, who stumbles and falls; Peter, who feels the piercing pain of his own failure.

> **"Pride goes before destruction,
> a haughty spirit before a fall."
> (Proverbs 16:18)**

Can you relate to *Peter*? Although he was a disciple within the inner circle of Jesus, *he* suffered *self-centered setbacks* that devastated him. He could have become paralyzed with despondency and despair, but one of the hallmarks of maturity is to evaluate our mistakes and wrong mind-sets and learn invaluable lessons from them. This way, our stumbling stones of failure can become stepping stones of success.

The root cause of an inability to accept failure and to learn from mistakes is a wrong belief system.

## ▶ WRONG BELIEF:

"Failure is a sign of personal defeat. I must accomplish my goals and be successful in the eyes of others to feel good about myself."

## ▶ RIGHT BELIEF:

"Failure is God's way of deepening my dependence on Him. Success is submitting to God's goal of Christlikeness for my life—regardless of the outcome."

**"We know that in all things God works for the good of those who love him, who have been called according to his purpose. For those God foreknew he also predestined to be conformed to the likeness of his Son, that he might be the firstborn among many brothers."
(Romans 8:28–29)**

# STEPS TO SOLUTION

*Three denials. Three questions.* There has to be a direct correlation.

It is the third time Jesus appears to the disciples following His resurrection. Peter and the other men have just finished breakfast on the beach with Jesus, enjoying bread and freshly caught fish and are warming over a charcoal fire. Suddenly and deliberately, Jesus turns His attention from the many to the one. His singular focus is Peter.

*"Do you truly love me more than these?"* Jesus asks.

Peter answers, *"Yes, Lord ... you know that I love you."*

Jesus then responds, *"Feed my lambs."*

A second time Jesus asks, *"Do you truly love me?"*

Peter answers again, *"Yes, Lord, you know that I love you."*

To which Jesus replies, *"Take care of my sheep."*

A third time, Jesus asks, *"Do you love me?"*

Peter's heart is grieved over the same question.

Why won't Jesus believe him?

Are his past failures too great? Will he ever get beyond not one, not two, but three denials of Jesus?

Nevertheless, Peter reaffirms his love, *"Lord, you know all things; you know that I love you."*

Though Jesus lovingly attempts to offset Peter's denials, it is Peter's future, a vital leadership role in the coming church, that preoccupies Jesus. *"Feed my sheep"* (John 21:15–17).

Perhaps Peter feared rebuke for past failures, but instead he finds restoration from his Lord. What a comfort for Peter—*and for you and me*!

## Key Verses to Memorize

▶ For the Moses personality who is extremely *fearful* of taking a risk:

"The one who calls you
is faithful and he will do it."
(1 Thessalonians 5:24)

▶ For the Peter personality who is totally *devastated* by failure:

"Peter came to Jesus and asked,
'Lord, how many times shall
I forgive my brother when he sins
against me? Up to seven times?'
Jesus answered, 'I tell you, not seven
times, but seventy-seven times.'"
(Matthew 18:21–22)

## Key Passage to Read

Good times, it seems, just don't get the job done. It's through the bad times that our faith is best honed. It's through the fiery trials that our testimony is forged.

Following the Crucifixion, Peter finds himself in the furnace of affliction—numerous times. Peter's personal failures—a result of his own pride and cowardice—prove he needs "purification."

In a chunk of unrefined gold, different impurities are emitted only at different temperatures. The refiner sloughs off the "dross"—the impurities—and then puts the crucible back into the fire and raises the temperature! Peter is like unrefined gold inside a furnace. God, the Refiner, uses the fire of "all kinds of trials" to purify Peter.

Ultimately, Peter comes forth as pure gold. And Peter says to his fellow sufferers around the world: *No trial will ever be wasted when put in the Refiner's hands.* Only after coming through the fire will they come forth as gold.

**"These have come so that your faith—of greater worth than gold, which perishes even though refined by fire—may be proved genuine and may result in praise, glory and honor when Jesus Christ is revealed." (1 Peter 1:7)**

### 1 Peter 5:6–10[15]

▶ **LET** your spirit be humble before God and others.

*"Humble yourselves, therefore, under God's mighty hand, that he may lift you up in due time."* (v. 6)

▶ **LEAVE** your fear and devastation in the hands of God.

"Cast all your anxiety on him because he cares for you." (v. 7)

▶ **LOCK** Satan outside the door of your mind.

"Be self-controlled and alert. Your enemy the devil prowls around like a roaring lion looking for someone to devour." (v. 8)

▶ **LEARN** the sweet fellowship of Christian suffering.

"Resist him, standing firm in the faith, because you know that your brothers throughout the world are undergoing the same kind of sufferings." (v. 9)

▶ **LOOK** to the God of grace to restore you.

"The God of all grace, who called you to his eternal glory in Christ, after you have suffered a little while, will himself restore you and make you strong, firm and steadfast." (v. 10)

We all have three God-given inner needs for love, for significance, and for security.[16] Clearly, when we look at Peter, so often he is trying to get his needs met for *significance*— but he goes about it the wrong way.

Evaluate what inner need is driving your outer need for success in a particular area. Is it **love**, **significance**, **security**, or some combination of the three? Realize that worldly success is generally rooted in our actions— what we do—while godly success is rooted in our character—*who we are*. God wants our "doing" to flow from who we are in Him, not from who we are without Him or from who we are just within ourselves.

If we are striving for success as a means to meet our inner needs that only He can truly meet, then we are "doing" in our own strength in order to meet our own needs. However, if we are looking to and relying on God to meet our needs, then we are free to "do" in His strength in order to accomplish His purposes.

When our needs are being taken care of by God, then we can truly focus on meeting the needs of others for their ultimate good rather than for our selfish gain.

> **"Everyone looks out for his own interests, not those of Jesus Christ." (Philippians 2:21)**

Since God made you with these basic inner needs, they obviously provide the fertile ground necessary for your spiritual growth. Jesus desires to make Himself known to you through your needs, and it is often through failure that those needs surface. In order to appropriate the adequacy of God, it is necessary for you to ...

▶ *Know* that you cannot meet your needs.

*"We do not want you to be uninformed, brothers, about the hardships we suffered in the province of Asia. We were under great pressure, far beyond our ability to endure, so that we despaired even of life."* (2 Corinthians 1:8)

▶ *Know* that your needs exist to expose your need of God.

*"Indeed, in our hearts we felt the sentence of death. But this happened that we might not rely on ourselves but on God, who raises the dead."* (2 Corinthians 1:9)

▶ *Know* that God planned to adopt you as His child.

*"In him was life, and that life was the light of men. ... Yet to all who received him, to those who believed in his name, he gave the right to become children of God—children born not of natural descent, nor of human decision or a husband's will, but born of God."* (John 1:4, 12–13)

▶ *Know* that Jesus is adequate to meet all your deepest needs.

*"He [Jesus] said to me, 'My grace is sufficient for you, for my power is made perfect in weakness.' Therefore I [Paul] will boast all the more gladly about my weaknesses, so that Christ's power may rest on me."* (2 Corinthians 12:9)

▶ *Know* that you can appropriate His adequacy.

*"I can do everything through him who gives me strength."* (Philippians 4:13)

▶ *Know* that you can thank Him for your inadequacy that you might experience His adequacy.

*"Give thanks in all circumstances, for this is God's will for you in Christ Jesus."* (1 Thessalonians 5:18)

▶ **_Know_** that God will work in and through you to accomplish His purposes in the lives of others.

*"It is God who works in you to will and to act according to his good purpose."* (Philippians 2:13)

▶ **_Know_** that God will continue to work in and through you until the day Christ returns.

*"Being confident of this, that he who began a good work in you will carry it on to completion until the day of Christ Jesus."* (Philippians 1:6)

"He had such promise, but it all ended in failure."

His fame spread, and expectations were raised. People followed Him by the droves, including Peter and the disciples. With their very eyes, they saw Jesus heal the hurting, feed the hungry, and transform sinners into "saints." People marveled at the mere carpenter—who manifested a wisdom that could come only from above.

But everything changed after three short years. Lofty expectations became instantly grounded. Jesus was sentenced to a criminal's death on a cross. "What a tragic end to the story!" some said then, and some still say today. But this death was no failure— certainly not on Jesus' part. It was the love, grace, justice, and power of God on full display, culminating in Jesus' resurrection.

The only failure surrounding the crucifixion story is one of comprehension: tragically misunderstanding, neglecting, and ignoring two eternally important questions: Why did Jesus have to die? and Why is His death relevant today? And the ultimate failure is when people neglect or refuse to put their faith in the Lord Jesus Christ, not allowing

Him to take control of their lives. The ultimate question for each of us is: How can you find God's forgiveness for your failures?

## How to Find God's Forgiveness for Your Failures

### #1 God's Purpose for You is *Salvation.*

What was the Father's motive in sending Jesus Christ to earth?

To save you through the fullest expression of His love!

*"God so loved the world, that he gave his one and only Son, that whoever believes in him should not perish but have eternal life. For God did not send his Son into the world to condemn the world, but to save the world through him."* (John 3:16–17)

What was Jesus' purpose in coming to earth?

To forgive your sins, empower you to have victory over sin, and enable you to live a fulfilled life!

*"I [Jesus] have come that they may have life, and have it to the full."* (John 10:10)

## #2 Your Problem is *Sin.*

What exactly is sin?

Sin is living *independently* of God's standard—knowing what is right, but failing to do what is right.

*"Anyone, then, who knows the good he ought to do and doesn't do it, sins."* (James 4:17)

What is the major consequence of sin?

Sin produces death, both spiritual and physical separation from God.

*"The wages of sin is death, but the gift of God is eternal life in Christ Jesus our Lord."* (Romans 6:23)

## #3 God's Provision for You is the *Savior.*

Can anything remove the penalty for sin?

Yes! Jesus died on the cross to personally pay the penalty for your sins.

*"God demonstrates his own love for us in this: While we were still sinners, Christ died for us."* (Romans 5:8)

What is the solution to being separated from God?

Trust in the person of Jesus Christ as being God in the flesh and in His death and resurrection as providing the only way to God the Father.

*"If you confess with your mouth, 'Jesus is Lord,' and believe in your heart that God raised him from the dead, you will be saved."* (Romans 10:9)

#### #4 Your Part is *Surrender.*

Place your faith in (rely on) Jesus Christ as your personal Lord and Savior and reject your "good works" as a means of gaining God's approval.

*"It is by grace you have been saved, through faith—and this not from yourselves, it is the gift of God—not by works, so that no one can boast."* (Ephesians 2:8–9)

Receive the blessings of being God's child and of the Spirit. The moment you trust in Jesus—He gives you His Spirit to live inside you.

*"You received the Spirit of sonship. ... The Spirit himself testifies with our spirit that we are God's children."* (Romans 8:15–16)

Then the Spirit of Christ enables you to live the fulfilled life God has planned for you, and He gives you His peace and power to heal from your failures and to learn from them. If you want to be fully forgiven by God and become the person God created you to be, you can tell Him in a simple, heartfelt prayer like this:

## PRAYER OF SALVATION

*"God, I want a real relationship with You. I admit that many times I've chosen to go my own way instead of Your way. Please forgive me for my sins. Jesus, thank You for dying on the cross to pay the penalty for my sins. Come into my life to be my Lord and my Savior. Change me from the inside out and make me the person You created me to be. In Your holy name I pray. Amen."*

## What Can You Expect Now?

By placing your trust in the completed work of Jesus Christ, look at what God says!

"His divine power has given us everything we need for life and godliness through our knowledge of him who called us by his own glory and goodness. Through these he has given us his very great and precious promises, so that through them you may participate in the divine nature and escape the corruption in the world caused by evil desires."
(2 Peter 1:3–4)

Because Peter was a man fully familiar with failure—sin, suffering, and setbacks—he also realized there were many others like him. That is why encouragement permeates the two letters in the Bible written by Peter, addressed to fellow believers suffering at that time—*and to you and me*. He urges us to stay the course, getting back up when we stumble and fall and going on in God's grace.

## OUR STUMBLING STONES CAN BECOME OUR STEPPING STONES TO SUCCESS!

Failures become foundational for success. As Peter learned firsthand ...

> "The God of all grace,
> who called you to his eternal glory in
> Christ, after you have suffered a little
> while, will himself restore you and make
> you strong, firm and steadfast."
> (1 Peter 5:10)

▶ The fact that you have failed doesn't make you a failure.

▶ Refuse to view failure as final.

▶ Expect failure to have consequences.

▶ Use failure as a stepping stone to success.

- ▶ Search for the good that God wants to bring out of failure.

- ▶ Research the lives of others who have failed.

- ▶ Realize that although you will fail, God will never fail you.

- ▶ Develop perseverance and never give up.

- ▶ If your failure is a result of sin, ask God's forgiveness.

- ▶ If your failure has hurt others, ask their forgiveness.

- ▶ If your failure has hurt you, accept God's forgiveness and move on.

- ▶ Recognize Satan as the source of inner accusation. He condemns; the Spirit gently convicts. And remember, Satan will still try to condemn even after sin has been confessed. The Bible describes Satan as, *"the accuser of our brothers, who accuses them before our God day and night"* (Revelation 12:10).

It is an ordinary day at the Beautiful Gate, and there lies the man lame from birth asking charity from those entering the temple. Peter and John are walking to the temple around 3:00 p.m. to pray. The lame man wants alms from the two apostles, yet he receives something even better. Peter says, *"Silver or gold I do not have, but what I have I give you. In the name of Jesus Christ of Nazareth, walk"* (Acts 3:6).

The lame man is healed, and crowds surround the two apostles. But Peter is troubled by the spotlight attention and communicates their total dependence on God for the miracle.

**"Men of Israel, why does this surprise you? Why do you stare at us as if by our own power or godliness we had made this man walk? ...**
**It is Jesus' name and the faith that comes through him that has given this complete healing to him,**
**as you can all see."**
**(Acts 3:12, 16)**

The Bible clearly states what we are to dwell on—what our minds should focus on. If we harness our thoughts so as not to live with anxiety, we can focus on the eight categories given to us in Philippians 4:8 as a guide. And we can turn each of these categories into a prayer.

## Dear Jesus, I Will Let My Mind Focus Only on What is ...

▶ *True*

"Although I've experienced pain in my past, I purpose to ignore Satan's lying accusations and focus on Your *truth*."

▶ *Noble*

"Since bitterness is really dishonoring to You, I release all of my bitterness out of *respect* for You."

▶ *Right*

"Although I am treated unjustly by others, I'm choosing to act in a way that is *right* in Your eyes toward others."

▶ *Pure*

"Although my heart hasn't always been pure, I will commit to a life that is *pure*."

▶ *Lovely*

"Even though others have shown disrespect, I will extend Jesus' *loving* respect."

### ▶ Admirable

"Even though I don't feel that others admire me, I want them to *admire* Christ."

### ▶ Excellent

"When my plans failed and I lost purpose, I learned to *excel* with Your plans and purpose."

### ▶ Praiseworthy

"When I feel defeated with no sense of worth, I know that Jesus is *praiseworthy* and my worth is in Him."

"Whatever is true,
whatever is noble,
whatever is right,
whatever is pure,
whatever is lovely,
whatever is admirable
—if anything is excellent
or praiseworthy
—think about such things."
(Philippians 4:8)

*Only one* from among the twelve did the angel specifically mention.

Mary Magdalene, Mary the mother of James, and Salome couldn't believe what they were seeing and hearing that morning following the Sabbath. They had brought spices to anoint the dead body of Jesus, but what they encountered was an empty tomb and a radiant messenger telling them Jesus had risen.

> "Go, tell his disciples and Peter,
> 'He is going ahead of you into Galilee.
> There you will see him,
> just as he told you.'"
> (Mark 16:7)

Tell his disciples and Peter, the angel directed. Peter, the disciple who professed Christ and denied Christ, who helped Jesus and hindered Jesus, runs to the tomb and when he sees burial clothes and no body, *"went away, wondering to himself what had happened"* (Luke 24:12).

## How Can You Turn From Failing in Life to Succeeding in Life?

▶**Return to Your First Love.**

- Pray that your heart will be totally in the hands of the Lord.

- Search God's Word. Read some of the Psalms each day—writing down each verse that focuses on your relationship with God.

- Turn your thoughts daily to the reality of your Lord's presence.

*"I hold this against you: You have forsaken your first love."* (Revelation 2:4)

▶**Recall Your Failure.**

- Write down each situation in which you have failed.

- Write out why you chose the course you took.

- Write out what you learned from each failure.

*"Remember the height from which you have fallen! Repent and do the things you did at first. If you do not repent, I will come to you and remove your lampstand from its place."* (Revelation 2:5)

## ▶ Repent through Godly Sorrow.

- Allow yourself to grieve over the results of your failure.

- Do not become defensive or "plead your own case."

- Know that godly sorrow leads to deeper growth.

*"Godly sorrow brings repentance that leads to salvation and leaves no regret, but worldly sorrow brings death."* (2 Corinthians 7:10)

## ▶ Receive God's Forgiveness.

- Know that God always comforts a repentant heart.

- Know that freedom is found only through accepting God's forgiveness.

- Accepting your freedom allows you to forgive others.

*"In you, O LORD, I have taken refuge; let me never be put to shame; deliver me in your righteousness. Turn your ear to me, come quickly to my rescue; be my rock of refuge, a strong fortress to save me."* (Psalm 31:1–2)

▶ **Respond Correctly to Brokenness.**

- Know that humility touches the heart of God.

- Be willing to admit that you need healthy brokenness.

- Admit your pain and sorrow.

*"The sacrifices of God are a broken spirit; a broken and contrite heart, O God, you will not despise."* (Psalm 51:17)

▶ **Remember God's Sovereignty.**

- Realize that God brings down and God lifts up.

- Realize that God is aware of all that happens to you.

- Realize that God will bring healing to your heart.

*"It is God who judges: He brings one down, he exalts another."* (Psalm 75:7)

▶ **Recognize God's Purpose.**

- God uses trials to grow you and to conform you to the character of Christ.

- God allows trials in your life to show your need of Him.

- God is refining you through your pain.

*"The LORD is righteous, he loves justice; upright men will see his face."* (Psalm 11:7)

## ▶ Realize Your Need for Christ.

- Know that apart from Christ, you can do nothing.

- Know that God can meet all your needs through Christ.

- Know that Christ is the source of all hope.

*"I am the vine; you are the branches. If a man remains in me and I in him, he will bear much fruit; apart from me you can do nothing."* (John 15:5)

## ▶ Refuse to Quit.

- Trust God even when you don't feel loved by God.

- Pick up your feet, shake off the dust, and start going to a Bible study.

- Respond correctly to your failure to build endurance.

*"Brothers, I do not consider myself yet to have taken hold of it. But one thing I do: Forgetting what is behind and straining toward what is ahead, I press on toward the goal to win the prize for which God has called me heavenward in Christ Jesus."* (Philippians 3:13–14)

▶ **Reach Out to Comfort Others.**

- Help others to see failure from God's perspective.

- Mentor others and share your experiences of failure and subsequent growth.

- Give devotionals, tracts, and biblical biographies to those who need God's comfort.

*"Praise be to the God and Father of our Lord Jesus Christ, the Father of compassion and the God of all comfort, who comforts us in all our troubles, so that we can comfort those in any trouble with the comfort we ourselves have received by God."* (2 Corinthians 1:3–4)

▶ **Rely on Christ within You.**

- Die to personal ambition and selfish gain and earnestly seek to know and glorify God.

- Fill your mind with the Word of God so that your thinking will line up with His thinking.

- Keep your mind and heart open to the scrutiny of the Holy Spirit so that you will be a clean and pure vessel for His use.

*"I have been crucified with Christ and I no longer live, but Christ lives in me. The life I live in the body, I live by faith in the Son of God, who loved me and gave himself for me."* (Galatians 2:20)

## WHAT TO Do When Someone Fails You

We all want it, but are we as willing to give it?

Grace—unmerited mercy, undeserved favor, unearned forgiveness—all abounding from the heart of God. And what has been poured onto us, we ought to, in turn, pour onto others.

But to be truthful, when someone fails us, all too often our gut reaction is to hold onto unforgiveness, to ruminate with resentment, and to subconsciously allow the root of bitterness to grow. When we feel "let down," often the first thing we ought to do is the last thing we want to do: *forgive!*

When we are struggling the most, when we just can't seem to get past our disappointments, remember that people failed Jesus too. We have all failed Jesus. Sobering, isn't it? And yet, He keeps on forgiving. Time and time again, our forgiving Savior models righteous behavior— even in the face of disappointment—and He rejoices when we are obedient in forgiveness and as we develop godly character.

Furthermore, when it comes to forgiving, we haven't been given a suggestion—we've been given a command:

> **"When you stand praying,
> if you hold anything against anyone,
> forgive him."**
> **(Mark 11:25)**

Scripture further tells us ...

> **"Be kind and compassionate
> to one another, forgiving each other,
> just as in Christ God forgave you."**
> **(Ephesians 4:32)**

But what if someone fails us time and time again? Are we really commanded to forgive time and time again? It is Peter who is feeling particularly generous when he makes this inquiry before Jesus. Religious leaders had instructed the Jewish people to forgive a person three times, but Peter asks Jesus if he should forgive up to seven times.

Jesus' response overflows with mercy, because to Him, even seven times is an inconceivably low number to aim for concerning forgiveness. *"I do not say to you, up to seven times, but up to seventy times seven"* (Matthew 18:22 NASB).

Jesus' point is not to forgive someone 490 times and then forever harden our hearts, He is communicating to us that we are to forgive endlessly and always. And what Jesus is communicating—we've already established—He also is commanding ...

> **"Whoever has my commands**
> **and obeys them,**
> **he is the one who loves me."**
> **(John 14:21)**

Peter had been the recipient of divine grace time and time again, and now he encourages his fellow strugglers to refrain from repaying evil with evil, insult with insult. He unveils the ultimate expression of the grace of God— grace that we are to pour onto others.

> **"Above all, love each other deeply,**
> **because love covers over**
> **a multitude of sins."**
> **(1 Peter 4:8)**

### ▶ Extend an outstretched hand.

*"Immediately Jesus reached out his hand and caught him. 'You of little faith,' he said, 'why did you doubt?'"* (Matthew 14:31)

► **Encourage conversation by asking questions.**

*"When they had finished eating, Jesus said to Simon Peter, 'Simon son of John, do you truly love me more than these?' 'Yes, Lord,' he said, 'you know that I love you.'"* (John 21:15)

► **Express the person's value to God.**

*"God so loved the world that he gave his one and only Son, that whoever believes in him shall not perish but have eternal life."* (John 3:16)

► **Entrust responsibility when appropriate.**

*"Jesus said, 'Feed my lambs.' ... Jesus said, 'Take care of my sheep.' ... Jesus said, 'Feed my sheep.'"* (John 21:15–17)

► **Explore a plan for achieving success in God's eyes.**

*"I urge you, brothers, in view of God's mercy, to offer your bodies as living sacrifices, holy and pleasing to God—this is your spiritual act of worship. Do not conform any longer to the pattern of this world, but be transformed by the renewing of your mind. Then you will be able to test and approve what God's will is—his good, pleasing and perfect will."* (Romans 12:1–2)

# Epilogue[17]

Jesus knew the end of the story. Despite the cycles of failure and success that characterized Peter's life, the impetuous apostle would finish well for his Lord. Just as Jesus predicted Peter's three denials, He also predicted that Peter would glorify God in a tragically beautiful way, upon a cross.

Jesus spoke these words to Peter: *"I tell you the truth, when you were younger you dressed yourself and went where you wanted; but when you are old you will stretch out your hands, and someone else will dress you and lead you where you do not want to go.' Jesus said this to indicate the kind of death by which Peter would glorify God. Then he said to him, 'Follow me!'"* (John 21:18–19).

Peter, the pastor of the early Christian Church in Jerusalem, was martyred around AD 67. Tradition tells us he requested to be hanged upside down on his cross because he didn't consider himself worthy to die in like manner of Jesus. Impetuous Peter became not only a humble man of God, but also a man greatly used by God.

Failure did not define the final chapter of Peter's life. Nor does it have to define ours. When we are feeling the most unworthy, the most useless, the most desperate, the most despairing, and when we have truly given up on ourselves, God hasn't. He longs to show us compassion and to encourage us to ultimately find success through failure.

Never allow your stumbling stones to forever knock you off your feet and immobilize you from meaningful service to God and others. Dust yourself off and begin to view those stumbling stones as stepping stones, constructively leading you down the path toward greater Christlikeness. And remember, whatever "successes" Peter experienced weren't achieved in his own strength, but in the strength of his God. Likewise, humble your heart and turn to God, who dearly loves you and desires to characterize your life by success!

"'For I know the plans I have for you,' declares the Lord, 'plans to prosper you and not to harm you, plans to give you hope and a future.'" (Jeremiah 29:11)

### NO ONE WHO IS FAITHFUL TO GOD IS A FAILURE

*The world honors success—
the Lord honors faithfulness.*

—June Hunt

# SCRIPTURES TO MEMORIZE

How do I overcome my fear of failure and face what I'm **called** to **do**?

*"The one who **calls** you is faithful and he will **do** it." (1 Thessalonians 5:24)*

How can I **lift** myself **up** out of the **humiliation** of failure?

*"**Humble** yourselves, therefore, under God's mighty hand, that he may **lift** you **up** in due time. Cast all your anxiety on him because he cares for you."*
*(1 Peter 5:6–7)*

What **things** can I **do** to recover from having **fallen** into sin and spiritual failure?

*"Remember the height from which you have **fallen**! Repent and **do** the **things** you did at first. If you do not repent, I will come to you and remove your lampstand from its place." (Revelation 2:5)*

Since God never fails at anything, doesn't He **despise** my failure and **brokenness**?

*"The sacrifices of God are a **broken** spirit; a **broken** and contrite heart, O God, you will not **despise**." (Psalm 51:17)*

How can I not fail when I feel **powerless** because of my **weaknesses**, and my abilities are **insufficient** to meet the need?

> *"He [Jesus] said to me, 'My grace is* ***sufficient*** *for you, for my power is made perfect in* ***weakness.***' *Therefore I [Paul] will boast all the more gladly about my weaknesses, so that Christ's* ***power*** *may rest on me. That is why, for Christ's sake, I delight in weaknesses, in insults, in hardships, in persecutions, in difficulties. For when I am weak, then I am strong."* *(2 Corinthians 12:9–10)*

My failure resulted in my life's being **torn to pieces**. Now what do I do with deep emotional **wounds**?

> *"Come, let us return to the* Lord. *He has* ***torn us to pieces*** *but he will heal us; he has injured us but he will bind up our* ***wounds.***" *(Hosea 6:1)*

Can **God work** in spite of my failures to somehow bring something **good** from them?

> *"We know that in all things* ***God works*** *for the* ***good*** *of those who love him, who have been called according to his purpose."* *(Romans 8:28)*

My pridefulness is a point of failure. How can I avoid **claiming credit for myself** in areas where I know I am **competent**?

*"Not that we are **competent** in ourselves **to claim anything for ourselves**, but our competence comes from God."*
*(2 Corinthians 3:5)*

### Can any **compassion** and **comfort** be found in the midst of **all my trouble**?

*"Praise be to the God and Father of our Lord Jesus Christ, the Father of **compassion** and the God of all **comfort**, who comforts us in **all our troubles**, so that we can comfort those in any trouble with the comfort we ourselves have received from God." (2 Corinthians 1:3–4)*

### Is it really possible to **forget** my failures by putting the past **behind** me?

*"Brothers, I do not consider myself yet to have taken hold of it. But one thing I do: **Forgetting** what is **behind** and straining toward what is ahead, I press on toward the goal to win the prize for which God has called me heavenward in Christ Jesus." (Philippians 3:13–14)*

# NOTES

1. *Webster's New World Dictionary*, 2nd college ed., s.v. "Fail."

2. James Strong, *The Exhaustive Concordance of the Bible: Showing Every Word of the Text of the Common English Version of the Canonical Books, and Every Occurrence of Each Word in Regular Order,* electronic edition, s.v. "Parar," (Ontario: Woodside Bible Fellowship, 1996).

3. *Webster's*, s.v. "Success."

4. Strong, *The Exhaustive Concordance of the Bible,* s.v. "Sakal."

5. Andre Bustanoby, *A Reason for Hope When You Have Failed* (San Bernardino, CA: Here's Life, 1986), 23–41, 53–60.

6. *A History of Wonderful Inventions* (London: Chapman and Hall, 1849), 77–78.

7. Michael Scott, *The Great Caruso* (New York: Knopf, A division of Random House, 1988), 6.

8. Kendall Haven and Donna Clark, *100 Most Popular Scientists for Young Adults: Biographical Sketches and Professional Paths* (Englewood, CO: Libraries Unlimited, 1999), 1163.

9. Nathan Miller, *New World Coming: The 1920s and the Making of Modern America* (New York: Scribner, 2003), 178.

10. Fred Charters Kelly, *The Wright Brothers: A Biography* (Toronto: Courier Dover, 1989), 153–154.

11. Ted Williams, *Ted Williams' Hit List: The Best of the Best Ranks the Best of the Rest* (New York: McGraw-Hill, 2003), 62.

12. Sir John Marks Templeton, *Discovering the Laws of Life* (New York: Templeton Foundation Press, 1995), 213.

13. Willie Jolley, *A Setback is a Setup for a Comeback: Turn you Moments of Doubt and Fear into Times of Triumph* (New York: St. Martin's Press, 1999), 26.

14. Bob Fenster, *Well, Duh! Our Stupid World, and Welcome to It* (Kansas City: Andrews McMeel, 2004), 286.

15. Bustanoby, *A Reason for Hope When You Have Failed*, 55–58.

16. Lawrence J. Crabb, Jr., *Understanding People: Deep Longings for Relationship*, Ministry Resources Library (Grand Rapids: Zondervan, 1987), 15–16; Robert S. McGee, *The Search for Significance*, 2nd ed. (Houston, TX: Rapha, 1990), 27–30.

17. Bustanoby, *A Reason for Hope When You Have Failed*, 59–60.

## SELECTED BIBLIOGRAPHY

Arthur, Kay. *As Silver Refined: Learning to Embrace Life's Disappointments.* Colorado Springs, CO: WaterBrook, 1997.

Beaudine, Frank R. *Ultimate Success.* Wheaton, IL: Tyndale House, 1997.

Berkley, James D. *Making the Most of Mistakes.* The Leadership Library, vol. 11. Carol Stream, IL: Word, 1987.

Briscoe, Jill. *How to Fail Successfully.* Old Tappan, NJ: Fleming H. Revell, 1982.

Briscoe, Jill. *How to Follow the Shepherd ... When You're Being Pushed Around by the Sheep.* Old Tappan, NJ: Power, 1982.

Brown, Stephen. *When Being Good Isn't Good Enough.* Nashville: Thomas Nelson, 1990.

Bustanoby, Andre. *A Reason for Hope When You Have Failed.* San Bernardino, CA: Here's Life, 1986.

Campolo, Anthony, Jr. *The Success Fantasy.* Wheaton, IL: Victor, 1980.

Crabb, Lawrence J., Jr. *Understanding People: Deep Longings for Relationship.* Ministry Resources Library. Grand Rapids: Zondervan, 1987.

Houtz, Elsa. *The Working Mother's Guide to Sanity.* Eugene, OR: Harvest House, 1989.

Hunt, June. *Seeing Yourself Through God's Eyes*. Eugene, OR: Harvest House, 2008.

Hunter, John E. *Limiting God: An Analysis of Christian Failure with the Sure Answer for Success*. Grand Rapids: Zondervan, 1966.

Johnson, Mark. *How to Succeed Where Strong Men Fail: Avoiding the Samson Trap*. Wheaton, IL: Harold Shaw, 1997.

Lutzer, Erwin W. *Conquering the Fear of Failure*. Ann Arbor, MI: Vine, 2002.

Lutzer, Erwin W. *Failure the Back Door to Success*. Chicago: Moody, 1975.

MacDonald, Gordon. *Rebuilding Your Broken World*. Nashville: Oliver-Nelson, 1988.

Manning, Brennan. *The Ragamuffin Gospel: Good News for the Bedraggled, Beat-up, and Burnt Out*. Portland, OR: Multnomah, 1990.

McGee, Robert S. *The Search for Significance*. 2nd ed. Houston, TX: Rapha, 1990.

Minirth, Frank, States V. Skipper, and Paul D. Meier. *100 Ways to Live a Happy and Successful Life*. Grand Rapids: Baker, 1979.

Scudder, James A. *Beyond Failure: Discovering Grace and Hope in the Hard Times of Life*. Wheaton, IL: Crossway, 2001.

Smith, Michael M. *Redeeming Failure.*
Discipleship Journal Bible Study. Colorado
Springs, CO: NavPress, 1999.

Stanley, Charles F. *Success God's Way.*
Nashville: Oliver-Nelson, 2000.

Wyrtzen, David. *Unexpected Grace: How
God Brings Meaning Out of Our Failures.*
Grand Rapids: Discovery House, 1992.

# HOPE FOR THE HEART TITLES

- *Adultery*
- *Aging Well*
- *Alcohol & Drug Abuse*
- *Anger*
- *Anorexia & Bulimia*
- *Boundaries*
- *Bullying*
- *Caregiving*
- *Chronic Illness & Disability*
- *Codependency*
- *Conflict Resolution*
- *Confrontation*
- *Considering Marriage*
- *Critical Spirit*
- *Decision Making*
- *Depression*
- *Domestic Violence*
- *Dysfunctional Family*
- *Envy & Jealousy*
- *Fear*
- *Financial Freedom*
- *Forgiveness*
- *Friendship*
- *Gambling*
- *Grief*
- *Guilt*
- *Hope*
- *Loneliness*
- *Manipulation*
- *Marriage*
- *Overeating*
- *Parenting*
- *Perfectionism*
- *Procrastination*
- *Reconciliation*
- *Rejection*
- *Self-Worth*
- *Sexual Integrity*
- *Singleness*
- *Spiritual Abuse*
- *Stress*
- *Success Through Failure*
- *Suicide Prevention*
- *Trials*
- *Verbal & Emotional Abuse*
- *Victimization*

**www.hendricksonrose.com**